FAMILY
FAVOURITES

Contents

Welcome!

Not only am I a dedicated and enthusiastic cook, but I love nothing more than encouraging those who think they are domestically challenged to pick up a pan and a spoon and get stirring. It doesn't take much to grasp the basics and from there, anything is possible. Hiding behind the mantra 'I can't cook' only brings fear into the kitchen, but it is these mistakes that will ultimately make you a better, more confident and knowledgeable cook. All it takes is some good recipes and plenty of enthusiasm and kitchen domination will surely follow. Luckily, all Good Housekeeping cookery books are filled with tempting recipes with clear methods and realistic photography – we are taking the chance out of cooking as our recipes are guaranteed to work.

If you have ever tried turning the page of a cookery book with dirty hands, while also balancing a steaming pan and a sticky spoon, then you will love the flip-chart design of this book. The simple fact that the recipes stand upright makes for an easier cooking experience – say goodbye to hovering over recipes while trying to stop the spoon dripping on to the pages.

This Good Housekeeping Flip It! book collection is filled with meticulously triple-tested recipes that have been developed and put through their paces in our dedicated test kitchens. We hope you enjoy the recipes and that they inspire you to give them a try – you know that they'll work after all!

Meike.

Meike Beck
Cookery Editor

Scrambled Eggs with Smoked Salmon

Serves 4

Preparation Time
10 minutes

Cooking Time
5 minutes

Per Serving
457 calories
33.9g fat
(of which 17.3g saturates)
17.2g carbohydrate
2.7g salt

6 large eggs
25g (1oz) butter, plus extra to spread
100g (3½oz) mascarpone
125g pack smoked salmon, sliced, or smoked
salmon trimmings
6 slices sourdough or rye bread, toasted, buttered
and cut into slim rectangles for soldiers
salt and ground black pepper

1 Crack the eggs into a jug and lightly beat together.
Season well.

2 Melt the butter in a non-stick pan over a low heat.
Add the eggs and stir constantly until the mixture
thickens. Add the mascarpone and season well. Cook for
1–2 minutes longer, until the mixture just becomes firm,
then fold in the smoked salmon. Serve at once with
toasted bread soldiers.

Gazpacho with Tortilla Chips

Serves 8
Preparation Time
25–30 minutes,
plus 2 hours or
overnight chilling

Per Serving
303 calories
20g fat
(of which 5g saturates)
28g carbohydrate
1.1g salt

Vegetarian

900g (2lb) ripe tomatoes
4 garlic cloves
50g (2oz) fresh white breadcrumbs
6 tbsp extra virgin olive oil
juice of 1½ small limes
1 red chilli, seeded and chopped (see Cook's Tips)
2 cucumbers, seeded and chopped
2 bunches spring onions, chopped
1 red pepper, seeded and chopped
600ml (1 pint) tomato juice
6 tbsp freshly chopped coriander
salt and ground black pepper
175g bag tortilla chips to serve

To garnish
1 large avocado
juice of ½ small lime
150ml (¼ pint) soured cream
a few fresh coriander sprigs

1 Score a cross in the skin at the base of each tomato, then put into a bowl. Pour over enough boiling water to cover them, leave for 30 seconds, then transfer to a bowl of cold water. Peel, discarding the skins, then cut into quarters. Discard the seeds.

2 Put all the gazpacho ingredients into a large bowl and mix well, then whiz together in batches in a food processor until smooth, and transfer to a bowl or jug. Season generously with salt and pepper and stir the soup well. Cover and chill for at least 2 hours or overnight.

3 Just before serving, peel and roughly dice the avocado, then toss in lime juice to coat. Serve the soup garnished with soured cream, the avocado, a sprinkling of black pepper and fresh coriander. Serve the tortilla chips separately.

Cook's Tips
Be extremely careful when handling chillies not to touch or rub your eyes with your fingers, as they will sting. Wash knives immediately after handling chillies for the same reason. As a precaution, use rubber gloves when preparing them if you like.
Don't be tempted to make the garnish too far in advance, as the delicate pale green flesh of avocado discolours when exposed to air.

French Toast

Serves 4
Preparation Time
5 minutes
Cooking Time
10 minutes

Per Finger
259 calories
19.6g fat
(of which 8.6g saturates)
15.2g carbohydrate
0.7g salt

Vegetarian

2 medium eggs
150ml (¼ pint) semi-skimmed milk
a generous pinch of freshly grated nutmeg or ground cinnamon
4 slices white bread, or fruit bread, crusts removed and each slice cut into four fingers
50g (2oz) butter
vegetable oil for frying
1 tbsp golden caster sugar

1 Beat the eggs, milk and nutmeg or cinnamon together in a shallow dish.

2 Dip the pieces of bread into the mixture, coating them well.

3 Heat half the butter with 1 tbsp oil in a heavy-based frying pan. When the butter is foaming, fry the egg-coated bread pieces in batches, until golden on both sides, adding more butter and oil as needed. Sprinkle with sugar to serve for brunch.

Cook's Tips
Use leftover bread for this tasty brunch dish.
For a savoury version, use white bread and omit the spice and sugar; serve with tomato ketchup, or with bacon and maple syrup.

Spanish Omelette

Serves 4
Preparation Time
15 minutes
Cooking Time
30–45 minutes

Per Serving
453 calories
25g fat
(of which 6g saturates)
38g carbohydrate
1.6g salt

900g (2lb) potatoes, peeled and left whole
3–4 tbsp vegetable oil
1 onion, finely sliced
8 medium eggs
3 tbsp chopped flat-leafed parsley
3 streaky bacon rashers
salt and ground black pepper
green salad to serve

1 Add the potatoes to a pan of cold salted water, bring to the boil, reduce the heat and simmer for 15–20 minutes or until almost cooked. Drain and leave until cool enough to handle, then slice thickly.

2 Heat 1 tbsp oil in an 18cm (7in) non-stick frying pan (suitable for use under the grill). Add the onion and fry gently for 7–10 minutes until softened; remove and set aside.

3 Lightly beat the eggs in a bowl and season well with salt and pepper.

4 Heat the remaining oil in the frying pan, then layer the potato slices, onion and 2 tbsp chopped parsley in the pan. Pour in the beaten eggs and cook for 5–10 minutes until the omelette is firm underneath. Meanwhile, grill the bacon until golden and crisp, then break into pieces.

5 Put the omelette in the pan under the grill for 2–3 minutes until the top is just set. Scatter the bacon and remaining chopped parsley over the surface. Serve cut into wedges, with a green salad.

Mixed Mushroom Frittata

Serves 4
Preparation Time
15 minutes
Cooking Time
15–20 minutes

Per Serving
148 calories
12g fat
(of which 3g saturates)
0g carbohydrate
0.3g salt

Vegetarian
Gluten Free Dairy Free

1 tbsp olive oil
300g (11oz) mixed mushrooms, sliced
2 tbsp freshly chopped thyme
zest and juice of ½ lemon
50g (2oz) watercress, chopped
6 medium eggs, beaten
salt and ground black pepper

1 Heat the oil in a large deep frying pan over a medium heat. Add the mushrooms and thyme, and stir-fry for 4–5 minutes until starting to soften and brown. Stir in the lemon zest and juice, then bubble for 1 minute. Reduce the heat.

2 Preheat the grill. Add the watercress to the beaten eggs, season with salt and pepper and pour into the pan. Cook on the hob for 7–8 minutes until the sides and base are firm but the centre is still a little soft.

3 Transfer to the grill and cook for 4–5 minutes until just set. Cut into wedges and serve with chunks of stoneground wholegrain bread and a crisp green salad.

Spicy Beans with Jazzed-up Potatoes

Serves 4

Preparation Time
Time 12 minutes

Cooking Time
about 1½ hours

Per Serving
298 calories
4g fat
(of which 1g saturates)
56g carbohydrate
0.8g salt

Gluten Free

4 baking potatoes
1 tbsp olive oil, plus extra to rub
1 tsp smoked paprika, plus a pinch
2 shallots, finely chopped
1 tbsp freshly chopped rosemary
400g can cannellini beans, drained and rinsed
400g can chopped tomatoes
1 tbsp light muscovado sugar
1 tsp Worcestershire sauce
75ml (2½fl oz) red wine
75ml (2½fl oz) hot vegetable stock
a small handful of freshly chopped
flat-leafed parsley
grated mature Cheddar cheese to sprinkle
salt and ground black pepper

1 Preheat the oven to 200°C (180°C fan oven) mark 6. Rub the baking potatoes with a little oil and put them on a baking tray. Scatter some sea salt over and a pinch of smoked paprika. Bake for 1–1½ hours.

2 Meanwhile, heat 1 tbsp oil in a large pan, then fry the shallots over a low heat for 1–2 minutes until they start to soften.

3 Add the rosemary and 1 tsp paprika, and fry for 1–2 minutes, then add the beans, tomatoes, sugar, Worcestershire sauce, red wine and stock. Season, then bring to the boil, reduce the heat and simmer, uncovered, for 10–15 minutes. Serve with the baked potatoes, scattered with chopped parsley and grated Cheddar cheese.

Try Something Different
The spicy beans are just as good served with toast for a quick meal that takes less than 25 minutes.

Cheesy Potato Pie

Serves 4
Preparation Time
10 minutes
Cooking Time
50 minutes

Per Serving
460 calories
21g fat
(of which 12g saturates)
52g carbohydrate
1.7g salt

900g (2lb) potatoes, peeled and cut into
even-sized chunks
3 tbsp milk
125g (4oz) Cotswold or Cheddar cheese,
grated (see Cook's Tip)
50g (2oz) butter
450g (1lb) leeks, trimmed and sliced
1 large red pepper, cored, seeded and
roughly chopped
450g (1lb) courgettes, thickly sliced
225g (8oz) button mushrooms
2 tsp mild paprika
25g (1oz) plain wholemeal flour
300ml (½ pint) vegetable stock
salt and ground black pepper

1 Preheat the oven to 200°C (180°C fan oven) mark 6. Cook the potatoes in lightly salted boiling water for 15–20 minutes until tender. Drain and mash with the milk, half the cheese and half the butter. Season to taste.

2 Meanwhile, heat the remaining butter in a large pan and fry the leeks and red pepper for 4–5 minutes until softened. Add the courgettes, mushrooms and paprika and fry for a further 2 minutes.

3 Sprinkle in the flour, then gradually add the stock and bring to the boil, stirring continuously. Cover and simmer for 5 minutes.

4 Spoon the vegetable mixture into an ovenproof serving dish and cover evenly with the cheesy potato. Sprinkle with the remaining cheese. Cook in the oven for 20–25 minutes until the top is crisp and golden brown.

Cook's Tip

Some vegetarians prefer to avoid cheeses that have been produced by the traditional method, because this uses animal-derived rennet. However, most supermarkets and cheese shops now stock an excellent range of vegetarian cheeses, produced using vegetarian rennet. Always check the label when buying.

Bacon & Egg Salad

Serves 4
Preparation Time
10 minutes
Cooking Time
10 minutes

Per Serving
360 calories
27g fat
(of which 8g saturates)
9g carbohydrate
3.1g salt

4 medium eggs
250g (9oz) rindless smoked bacon
150g (5oz) cherry tomatoes
2 slices thick-cut bread
3 tbsp mayonnaise
½ lemon
25g (1oz) freshly grated Parmesan
2 Little Gem lettuces
ground black pepper

1 Heat a pan of water until simmering, add the eggs and boil for 6 minutes. Cool completely under cold water, peel and set to one side.

2 Meanwhile, heat a griddle pan, then fry the bacon for 5 minutes until crisp. Remove from the pan and chop into large pieces. Leave to cool.

3 Add the tomatoes and bread to the pan and fry in the bacon juices for 2–3 minutes until the bread is crisp and the tomatoes are starting to char. Remove from the heat, chop the bread into bite-sized croûtons and set to one side.

4 To make the dressing, put the mayonnaise into a bowl and squeeze in the lemon juice. Add the Parmesan to the bowl and mix. Season with pepper.

5 Separate the Little Gem leaves and put into a large serving bowl. Cut the eggs in half and add to the bowl with the bacon, tomatoes and croûtons. Drizzle the dressing over, toss lightly and serve.

Warm Spicy Chorizo & Chickpea Salad

Serves 6
Preparation Time
15 minutes
Cooking Time
about 15 minutes

Per Serving
365 calories
23.5g fat
(of which 5.7g saturates)
27g carbohydrate
1.3g salt

Dairy Free

5 tbsp olive oil
200g (7oz) chorizo or spicy sausage, thinly sliced
225g (8oz) red onion, chopped
1 large red pepper, seeded and roughly chopped
3 garlic cloves, finely chopped
1 tsp cumin seeds
2 × 400g cans chickpeas, drained and rinsed
2 tbsp freshly chopped coriander
juice of 1 lemon
salt and ground black pepper

1 Heat 1 tbsp olive oil in a non-stick frying pan and cook the chorizo or spicy sausage over a medium heat for 1–2 minutes until lightly browned. Remove the chorizo with a slotted spoon and put to one side. Fry the onion in the chorizo oil for 8–10 minutes or until browned.

2 Add the red pepper, garlic, cumin and chickpeas to the onion and cook for a further 5 minutes, stirring frequently to prevent sticking. Remove the pan from the heat and add the chorizo.

3 Add the coriander, lemon juice and remaining olive oil. Season well and serve immediately.

Chickpea & Chilli Stir-fry

Serves 4
Preparation Time
10 minutes
Cooking Time
15-20 minutes

Per Serving
258 calories
11g fat
(of which 1g saturates)
30g carbohydrate
1g salt

Vegetarian
Gluten Free Dairy Free

2 tbsp olive oil
1 tsp ground cumin
1 red onion, sliced
2 garlic cloves, finely chopped
1 red chilli, seeded and finely chopped
(see Cook's Tips page 7)
2 × 400g cans chickpeas, drained and rinsed
400g (14oz) cherry tomatoes
125g (4oz) baby spinach leaves
salt and ground black pepper
rice or pasta to serve

1 Heat the oil in a wok or large frying pan. Add the cumin and fry for 1-2 minutes. Add the onion and stir-fry for 5-7 minutes.

2 Add the garlic and chilli and stir-fry for 2 minutes.

3 Add the chickpeas to the wok with the tomatoes. Reduce the heat and simmer until the chickpeas are hot. Season with salt and pepper. Add the spinach and cook for 1-2 minutes until the leaves have wilted. Serve with rice or pasta.

Five-minute Stir-fry

Serves 2
Preparation Time
2 minutes
Cooking Time
5 minutes

Per Serving
170 calories
7g fat
(of which 1g saturates)
11g carbohydrate
1.6g salt

Gluten Free Dairy Free

1 tbsp sesame oil
175g (6oz) raw peeled tiger prawns, deveined
(see Cook's Tip)
50ml (2fl oz) ready-made sweet chilli and
ginger sauce
225g (8oz) ready-prepared mixed stir-fry
vegetables, such as sliced courgettes, broccoli
and green beans

1 Heat the oil in a large wok or frying pan, add the prawns and sweet chilli and ginger sauce and stir-fry for 2 minutes.

2 Add the mixed vegetables and stir-fry for a further 2–3 minutes until the prawns are cooked and the vegetables are heated through. Serve immediately.

Try Something Different
Instead of prawns, try chicken cut into strips: stir-fry for 5 minutes in step 1.

Cook's Tip
To devein prawns, pull off the head and discard (or put to one side and use later for making stock). Using pointed scissors, cut through the soft shell on the belly side. Prise off the shell, leaving the tail attached. (The shell can also be used later for making stock.) Using a small sharp knife, make a shallow cut along the back of the prawn. Using the point of the knife, remove and discard the black vein (the intestinal tract) that runs along the back of the prawn.

Red Onion Tarte Tatin

Serves 12

Preparation Time

15 minutes

Cooking Time

35-40 minutes

Per Serving

235 calories

15g fat

(of which 3g saturates)

23g carbohydrate

0.4g salt

Vegetarian

50g (2oz) butter

2 tbsp olive oil

1.1kg (2½lb) red onions, sliced into rounds

1 tbsp light muscovado sugar

175ml (6fl oz) white wine

4 tsp white wine vinegar

1 tbsp freshly chopped thyme, plus extra to garnish (optional)

450g (1lb) puff pastry

plain flour to dust

salt and ground black pepper

1 Lightly grease two 23cm (9in) non-stick sandwich tins with a little of the butter and set aside.

2 Melt the remaining butter with the oil in a large non-stick frying pan. Add the sliced onions and sugar, and fry for 10-15 minutes or until golden, keeping the onions in their rounds.

3 Preheat the oven to 220°C (200°C fan) mark 7. Add the wine, vinegar and thyme to the pan. Bring to the boil, and let it bubble until the liquid has evaporated. Season with salt and pepper, then divide the mixture between the tins and leave to cool.

4 Halve the pastry. On a lightly floured surface, roll out each piece thinly into a round shape just larger than the sandwich tin. Put one pastry round over the onion mixture in each tin and tuck in the edges. Prick the pastry dough all over with a fork.

5 Cook the tarts for 15-20 minutes or until the pastry is risen and golden. Take out of the oven and put a large warm plate over the pastry. Turn over and shake gently to release the tart, then remove the tin. Scatter with thyme, if you like, and cut into wedges to serve.

Get Ahead

Complete the recipe to the end of step 4 up to one day in advance. Cover and keep in the fridge for up to 24 hours. To use, complete the recipe.

Sausage Rolls

Makes 28
Preparation Time
25 minutes
Cooking Time
30 minutes

Per Serving
119 calories
9g fat
(of which 2g saturates)
8g carbohydrate
0.4g salt

450g (1lb) puff pastry, thawed if frozen
plain flour to dust
450g (1lb) pork sausage meat
milk to brush
beaten egg to glaze

1 Preheat the oven to 220°C (200°C fan oven) mark 7. Roll out half the puff pastry on a lightly floured surface to a 40.5 × 20.5cm (16 × 8in) rectangle; cut lengthways into two strips.

2 Divide the sausage meat into four, dust with flour and form two portions into rolls, the length of the pastry. Lay a sausage-meat roll on each strip of pastry. Brush the pastry edges with a little milk, fold one side of the pastry over and press the long edges together to seal. Repeat with the remaining pastry and sausage meat. Trim the ends.

3 Brush the pastry with beaten egg to glaze and cut each roll into 5cm (2in) lengths. Make two or three slits in the top of each one.

4 Transfer to a baking sheet and cook in the oven for 15 minutes. Reduce the oven temperature to 180°C (160°C fan oven) mark 4 and cook for a further 15 minutes. Transfer to a wire rack. Serve hot or cold.

Try Something Different
Add 1 hot red chilli, seeded and finely chopped (see Cook's Tip, page 7), 1 tbsp freshly grated ginger and a handful of freshly chopped coriander leaves to the pork sausage meat.

Deli Pizza

Serves 4
Preparation Time
5 minutes
Cooking Time
15 minutes

Per Serving
440 calories
15g fat
(of which 5g saturates)
64g carbohydrate
2.8g salt

Vegetarian

6 tbsp fresh tomato sauce (see Cook's Tip)
2 pizzeria-style pizza bases
100g (3½oz) soft goat's cheese
1 red onion, finely sliced
100g (3½oz) sunblush tomatoes
100g (3½oz) pitted black olives
a handful of fresh basil, roughly torn
green salad to serve

1 Preheat the oven to 220°C (200°C fan oven) mark 7. Put a large baking sheet on the top shelf to heat up.

2 Spread a thin layer of the tomato sauce over each of the pizza bases, leaving a 2.5cm (1in) border around the edge. Top with dollops of goat's cheese, then scatter on the onion, tomatoes and olives.

3 Slide one of the pizzas on to the hot baking sheet and bake for 15 minutes or until golden and crisp. Repeat with the second pizza base. Scatter the torn basil over each pizza and serve immediately with a green salad.

Try Something Different
Try marinated peppers, artichokes or chargrilled aubergines instead of the olives and sunblush tomatoes.

Cook's Tip
Fresh pasta sauce To make a fresh tomato sauce, put 900g (2lb) roughly chopped vine-ripened tomatoes into a pan with 2 tbsp extra virgin olive oil, 2 crushed garlic cloves, the grated zest of 1 lemon and 1 tsp dried oregano. Bring to the boil, cover and simmer gently for 20 minutes. Add 2 tbsp freshly chopped basil, salt and ground black pepper to taste and a little sugar if required. Simmer, uncovered, for a further 10 minutes or until the sauce is slightly thickened. If you like a smooth sauce, pass through a sieve and reheat before serving.

Mozzarella, Parma Ham & Rocket Pizza

Serves 4
Preparation Time
10 minutes
Cooking Time
15–18 minutes

Per Serving
508 calories
19g fat
(of which 11g saturates)
64g carbohydrate
1.9g salt

a little plain flour to dust
290g pack pizza base mix
350g (12oz) fresh tomato and chilli pasta sauce
250g (9oz) buffalo mozzarella cheese, drained and roughly chopped
6 slices Parma ham, torn into strips
50g (2oz) rocket
a little extra virgin olive oil to drizzle
salt and ground black pepper

1 Preheat the oven to 200°C (180°C fan oven) mark 6 and lightly flour two large baking sheets. Mix the pizza base dough according to the pack instructions. Divide the dough into two and knead each ball on a lightly floured surface for about 5 minutes, then roll them out to make two 23cm (9in) rounds. Put one on each of the prepared baking sheets.

2 Divide the tomato sauce between the pizza bases and spread it over, leaving a small border around each edge. Scatter on the mozzarella pieces, then scatter with ham. Season well with salt and pepper.

3 Cook the pizzas for 15–18 minutes until golden. Slide on to a wooden board, top with rocket leaves and drizzle with oil. Cut in half to serve.

Cook's Tip
If you're short of time, buy two ready-made pizza bases.

Macaroni Cheese

Serves 4
Preparation Time
10 minutes
Cooking Time
15 minutes

Per Serving
680 calories
34g fat
(of which 21g saturates)
67g carbohydrate
2g salt

Vegetarian

225g (8oz) short-cut macaroni
50g (2oz) butter
50g (2oz) plain flour
900ml (1½ pints) milk
½ tsp grated nutmeg or mustard powder
225g (8oz) mature Cheddar cheese, grated
3 tbsp fresh white or wholemeal breadcrumbs
salt and ground black pepper

1 Cook the macaroni in a large pan of lightly salted boiling water, according to the pack instructions, until al dente.

2 Meanwhile, melt the butter in a pan, stir in the flour and cook, stirring, for 1 minute. Remove from the heat and gradually stir in the milk. Bring to the boil and cook, stirring, until the sauce thickens. Remove from the heat. Season with salt and pepper, and add the grated nutmeg or mustard.

3 Drain the macaroni and add to the sauce, together with three-quarters of the cheese. Mix well, then turn into an ovenproof dish.

4 Preheat the grill to high. Sprinkle the breadcrumbs and remaining cheese over the macaroni. Put under the grill for 2–3 minutes until golden brown on top and bubbling. Serve.

Tagliatelle Carbonara

Serves 4	350g (12oz) tagliatelle
Preparation Time	150g (5oz) smoked bacon, chopped
5 minutes	1 tbsp olive oil
Cooking Time	2 large egg yolks
10 minutes	150ml (¼ pint) double cream
	50g (2oz) freshly grated Parmesan
Per Serving	2 tbsp freshly chopped parsley
688 calories	salt
39g fat	
(of which 19g saturates)	
65g carbohydrate	
1.6g salt	

1 Cook the pasta in a large pan of lightly salted boiling water according to the pack instructions. Drain.

2 Meanwhile, fry the bacon in the oil for 4–5 minutes. Add to the drained pasta and keep hot.

3 Put the egg yolks into a bowl, add the cream and whisk together. Add to the pasta with the Parmesan and parsley, toss well and serve.

Classic Lasagne

Serves 6
Preparation Time
40 minutes
Cooking Time
45 minutes
(without the
Bolognese Sauce)

Per Serving
367 calories
14g fat
(of which 5g saturates)
36g carbohydrate
1.9g salt

1 quantity Bolognese Sauce (see page 33)
butter to grease
350g (12oz) fresh lasagne, or 225g (8oz)
'no need to pre-cook' dried lasagne
(see Cook's Tips) (12–15 sheets)
1 quantity Béchamel Sauce (see Cook's Tips)
3 tbsp freshly grated Parmesan
salad leaves to serve

1 Preheat the oven to 180°C (160°C fan oven) mark 4. Spoon one-third of the Bolognese Sauce over the base of a greased 2.3 litre (4 pint) ovenproof dish. Cover with a layer of lasagne sheets, then a layer of Béchamel sauce. Repeat these layers twice more, finishing with a layer of Béchamel to cover the lasagne.

2 Sprinkle the Parmesan over the top and stand the dish on a baking sheet. Cook in the oven for 45 minutes or until well browned and bubbling. Serve with salad leaves.

Cook's Tips

If using 'no need to pre-cook' dried lasagne, add a little extra stock or water to the sauce.

Béchamel sauce To make a béchamel sauce, pour 300ml (½ pint) semi-skimmed milk into a pan. Add 1 onion slice, 6 peppercorns, 1 mace and 1 bay leaf. Bring almost to the boil, remove from the heat, and cover and leave to infuse for about 20 minutes, then strain. To make the roux, melt 15g (½oz) butter in a pan, stir in 15g (½oz) plain flour and cook, stirring, for 1 minute until cooked but not coloured. Remove from the heat and gradually pour on the infused milk, whisking constantly. Season lightly with salt, pepper and grated nutmeg. Return to the heat and cook, stirring constantly, until the sauce is thickened and smooth. Simmer gently for 2 minutes. Makes 300ml (½ pint).

Spinach & Ricotta Cannelloni

Serves 4	1 tbsp olive oil, plus extra to oil
Preparation Time	1 small onion, chopped
25 minutes	1 bay leaf
Cooking Time	1 garlic clove, crushed
1 hour 10 minutes	400g can chopped tomatoes
	300g (11oz) spinach, coarse stalks removed
Per Serving	2 × 250g tubs ricotta cheese
409 calories	1 large egg
14g fat	25g (1oz) freshly grated Parmesan
(of which 7g saturates)	freshly grated nutmeg
53g carbohydrate	15 cannelloni tubes
1.5g salt	125g mozzarella ball, roughly pulled into small pieces
Vegetarian	salt and ground black pepper
	fresh basil leaves to garnish

1 Heat the oil in a pan and gently fry the onion with the bay leaf for 10 minutes or until softened. Add the garlic and fry for 1 minute. Pour in the tomatoes along with half a can of cold water, bring to the boil, then reduce the heat and simmer for 20 minutes or until slightly thickened.

2 Meanwhile, wash the spinach and put into a large pan set over a low heat. Cover the pan and cook the spinach for 2 minutes or until just wilted. Drain and cool under running water. When cool enough to handle, squeeze out the excess moisture and chop roughly.

3 Preheat the oven to 180°C (160°C fan oven) mark 4 and lightly oil a baking dish. Mix together the ricotta, egg, Parmesan and spinach with a grating of nutmeg and season with plenty of salt and pepper. Spoon or pipe into the cannelloni tubes and put into the dish in one layer.

4 Pour the tomato sauce over the pasta, then dot with the mozzarella. Bake for 30–40 minutes until golden and bubbling. Scatter with the basil and serve.

Cook's Tip
Usually made from egg pasta, cannelloni are large, broad tubes designed to be stuffed, coated in sauce and baked.

Spaghetti Bolognese

Serves 6
Preparation Time
15 minutes
Cooking Time
40 minutes

Per serving
510 calories
12g fat
(of which 4g saturates)
67g carbohydrate
1.5g salt

500g (1lb 2oz) dried spaghetti
50g (2oz) Parmesan, freshly grated

For the Bolognese sauce
2 tbsp olive oil
1 onion, finely chopped
2 garlic cloves, crushed
450g (1lb) extra-lean minced beef
2 tbsp sun-dried tomato paste
300ml (½ pint) red wine
400g can chopped tomatoes
125g (4oz) chestnut mushrooms, sliced
2 tbsp Worcestershire sauce
salt and ground black pepper

1 To make the Bolognese sauce, heat the oil in a large pan, add the onion and fry over a medium heat for 10 minutes or until softened and golden. Add the garlic and cook for 1 minute.

2 Add the minced beef and brown evenly, using a wooden spoon to break up the pieces. Stir in the tomato paste and the red wine, cover and bring to the boil. Add the tomatoes, mushrooms and Worcestershire sauce, and season well with salt and pepper. Bring back to the boil, reduce the heat and simmer for 20 minutes.

3 Cook the spaghetti in a large pan of lightly salted boiling water according to the pack instructions until al dente. Drain the pasta well, then return to the pan. Add the Bolognese sauce and toss to mix together. Check the seasoning.

4 Divide among warmed plates and sprinkle with the Parmesan to serve.

Try Something Different
Add 125g (4oz) chopped rinded smoked streaky bacon with the mince, brown, then stir in 200g (7oz) chopped chicken livers. Cook for 3 minutes before adding the tomato paste, then continue as above.

Old-fashioned Fish Pie

Serves 4	450g (1lb) haddock, cod or coley fillets
Preparation Time	300ml (½ pint) milk, plus 6 tbsp
20 minutes	1 bay leaf
Cooking Time	6 black peppercorns
50 minutes	2 onion slices
	65g (2½oz) butter
Per Serving	3 tbsp flour
610 calories	150ml (¼ pint) single cream
28g fat	2 medium eggs, hard-boiled, shelled and chopped
(of which 15g saturates)	2 tbsp freshly chopped flat-leafed parsley
56g carbohydrate	900g (2lb) potatoes, cooked and mashed
1.4g salt	1 medium egg
	salt and ground black pepper

1 Put the fish into a frying pan, pour the 300ml (½ pint) milk over it and add the bay leaf, peppercorns, onion slices and a good pinch of salt. Bring slowly to the boil, cover, reduce the heat and simmer for 8–10 minutes until the fish flakes when tested with a fork.

2 Using a fish slice, lift the fish out of the pan and put on a plate. Flake the fish, discarding the skin and bone. Strain and put the milk to one side. Preheat the oven to 200°C (180°C fan oven) mark 6.

3 Melt 40g (1½oz) of the butter in a pan, stir in the flour and cook gently for 1 minute, stirring. Remove the pan from the heat and gradually stir in the reserved milk. Bring to the boil slowly and continue to cook, stirring until the sauce thickens. Season.

4 Stir in the cream and fish, together with any juices. Add the chopped eggs and parsley and adjust the seasoning. Spoon the mixture into a 1.1 litre (2 pint) pie dish or similar ovenproof dish.

5 Heat 6 tbsp milk and remaining butter in a pan, then beat into the potatoes. Season. Leave to cool slightly.

6 Spoon the cooled potato into a large piping bag fitted with a large star nozzle. Pipe shell-shaped lines of potato across the fish mixture. Alternatively, spoon potato on top and roughen the surface with a fork.

7 Put the dish on a baking sheet and cook in the oven for 10–15 minutes until the potato is set.

8 Beat the egg with a good pinch of salt, then brush over the pie. Return to the oven for 15 minutes or until golden brown.

Try something different
- Stir 125g (4oz) grated Cheddar cheese into the sauce.
- Beat 125g (4oz) grated Cheddar or Red Leicester cheese into the mashed potatoes.
- Stir 175g (6oz) canned sweetcorn, drained, and ¼ tsp cayenne pepper into the fish mixture.
- Fry 125g (4oz) sliced button mushrooms in 25g (1oz) butter for 3 minutes. Stir into the fish mixture.
- Sprinkle the potato topping with 50g (2oz) mixed grated Parmesan and fresh breadcrumbs after the first 10–15 minutes.
- Cover the pie with puff pastry instead of the potatoes.

Simple Paella

Serves 6

Preparation Time
15 minutes,
plus infusing

Cooking Time
50 minutes

Per Serving
568 calories
18g fat
(of which 3g saturates)
61g carbohydrate
2.5g salt

Gluten Free Dairy Free

1 litre (1¾ pints) chicken stock
½ tsp saffron threads
5 tbsp extra virgin olive oil
6 boneless, skinless chicken thighs, each cut into
three pieces
1 large onion, chopped
4 large garlic cloves, crushed
1 tsp paprika
2 red peppers, seeded and sliced
400g can chopped tomatoes
350g (12oz) long-grain rice
200ml (7fl oz) dry sherry
500g (1lb 2oz) cooked mussels
200g (7oz) cooked and peeled tiger prawns
juice of ½ lemon
salt and ground black pepper
lemon wedges and fresh flat-leafed parsley to serve

1 Heat the stock, then add the saffron and leave to infuse for 30 minutes.

2 Heat half the oil in a frying pan and fry the chicken in batches for 3–5 minutes until golden brown. Set the chicken aside. Lower the heat slightly. Add the remaining oil. Fry the onion for 5 minutes or until soft. Add the garlic and paprika, and stir for 1 minute. Add the chicken, red peppers and tomatoes. Stir in the rice. Add one-third of the stock and bring to the boil. Season with salt and pepper. Reduce the heat to a simmer. Cook, uncovered, stirring continuously, until most of the liquid has been absorbed.

3 Add the remaining stock a little at a time, letting the rice absorb it before adding more. (This should take about 25 minutes.) Add the sherry and cook for 2 minutes – the rice should be quite wet, as it will continue to absorb liquid. Add the mussels and prawns, with their juices, and the lemon juice. Stir in and cook for 5 minutes to heat through. Adjust the seasoning and serve with lemon wedges and parsley.

Cook's Tip
Ready-cooked mussels are available vacuum-packed from supermarkets. Alternatively, to cook from fresh, rinse under cold running water, scrub the shells thoroughly to remove any barnacles then pull off the hairy beard.
Tap any open mussels sharply with the back of the knife and if they refuse to close discard. Put the mussels in a large pan and add 50ml (2fl oz) water. Cover with a tight-fitting lid and cook for 3–4 minutes, shaking the pan occasionally, until the mussels open. Transfer to a bowl, discard any unopened mussels, and keep the cooking liquid to one side.

Fish & Chips

Serves 2

Preparation Time
15 minutes

Cooking Time
12 minutes

Per Serving
1186 calories
79g fat
(of which 18g saturates)
73g carbohydrate
3.2g salt

4 litres (7 pints) sunflower oil for deep-frying
125g (4oz) self-raising flour
¼ tsp baking powder
¼ tsp salt
1 medium egg
150ml (¼ pint) sparkling mineral water
2 hake fillets, about 125g (4oz) each
450g (1lb) Desirée potatoes, peeled and
cut into 1cm (½in) chips
salt, vinegar and lemon mayonnaise
(see Cook's Tip) to serve

1 Heat the oil in a deep-fryer to 190°C (test by frying a small cube of bread – it should brown in 20 seconds).

2 Whiz the flour, baking powder, salt, egg and water in a food processor or blender until combined into a batter. Remove the blade from the food processor. (Alternatively, put the ingredients into a bowl and beat everything together until smooth.) Drop one of the fish fillets into the batter to coat it.

3 Put half the chips into the deep-fryer, then add the battered fish. Fry for 6 minutes or until just cooked, then remove and drain well on kitchen paper. Keep warm if not serving immediately.

4 Drop the remaining fillet into the batter to coat, then repeat step 3 with the remaining chips. Serve with salt, vinegar and lemon mayonnaise.

Cook's Tip
Lemon Mayonnaise Put 2 medium egg yolks, 2 tsp lemon juice, 1 tsp Dijon mustard and a pinch of sugar into a food processor. Season, then whiz briefly until pale and creamy. With the motor running, slowly pour in 300ml (½ pint) light olive oil through the feeder tube, in a steady stream, until the mayonnaise is thick. Add 1 tsp grated lemon zest and an additional 1 tbsp lemon juice and whiz briefly to combine. Store the mayonnaise in a screw-topped jar in the fridge. It will keep for up to three days.

Fishcakes

Serves 4
Preparation Time
15 minutes
Cooking Time
20 minutes

Per Serving
412 calories
19g fat
(of which 5g saturates)
39g carbohydrate
1.5g salt

350g (12oz) fish, such as cod, haddock or coley,
cooked and flaked
350g (12oz) potatoes, cooked and mashed
25g (1oz) butter
1 tbsp freshly chopped flat-leafed parsley
a few drops of anchovy essence (optional)
milk, if needed
1 medium egg, beaten
plain flour to dust
125g (4oz) fresh breadcrumbs
vegetable oil for shallow-frying
salt and ground black pepper
basil leaves to garnish
lemon wedges and salad to serve

1 Mix the fish with the potatoes, butter, parsley,
seasoning and anchovy essence, if using, binding
if necessary with a little milk or beaten egg.

2 On a lightly floured board, form the mixture into
a roll, then cut into eight slices and shape into flat
cakes. Coat them with egg and breadcrumbs.

3 Heat the oil in a frying pan, add the fishcakes and fry,
turning once, until crisp and golden. Drain well on
kitchen paper. Garnish with basil and serve with lemon
wedges and salad.

Try something different
Replace the cod, haddock or coley with smoked haddock,
herrings, canned tuna or salmon.

Fish Goujons

Serves 4
Preparation Time
15 minutes
Cooking Time
10 minutes

Per serving
267 calories
15g fat
(of which 2g saturates)
10g carbohydrate
0.6g salt

450g (1lb) hake fillets, skinned, boned
and cut into 20 even-sized pieces
1 medium egg, beaten
50g (2oz) fresh breadcrumbs
vegetable oil for deep-frying
tartare sauce to serve

1 Coat the fish pieces in egg, then in the breadcrumbs.

2 Heat the oil in a deep-fat fryer to 180°C (test by frying a small cube of bread; it should brown in 40 seconds), add the fish and fry until golden. Drain on kitchen paper.

3 Serve the goujons on cocktail sticks with the sauce handed separately.

Try Something Different
Other firm fish such as haddock, coley, cod, monkfish and huss can be cooked in the same way.

Cod with Cherry Tomatoes

Serves 4

Preparation Time

15 minutes

Cooking Time

20-25 minutes

Per Serving

168 calories

7g fat

(of which 1g saturates)

8g carbohydrate

0.2g salt

Dairy Free

4 × 100g (3½oz) cod steaks
1 tbsp plain flour
2 tbsp olive oil
1 small onion, sliced
1 large red chilli, seeded and chopped
(see Cook's Tips page 7)
1 garlic clove, crushed
250g (9oz) cherry tomatoes, halved
4 spring onions, chopped
2 tbsp freshly chopped coriander
salt and ground black pepper

1 Season the cod with salt and pepper, then dust lightly with the flour. Heat 1 tbsp oil in a large frying pan, add the onion and fry for 5-10 minutes until golden.

2 Pour the remaining oil into the pan. Add the cod and fry for 3 minutes on each side. Add the chilli, garlic, cherry tomatoes, spring onions and coriander and season with salt and pepper. Cover and continue to cook for 5-10 minutes until everything is heated through. Serve immediately.

Try Something Different
Use another white fish such as sea bass or pollack fillets instead of the cod.

Oxford Sausages

Makes about 18

Preparation Time

20 minutes

Cooking Time

20 minutes

Per Serving

267 calories

19g fat

(of which 10g saturates)

12g carbohydrate

0.6g salt

450g (1lb) lean boneless pork, minced or very finely chopped

450g (1lb) lean boneless veal, minced or very finely chopped

350g (12oz) shredded suet

225g (8oz) fresh breadcrumbs

grated zest of ½ lemon

1 tsp freshly grated nutmeg

2 tbsp freshly chopped mixed herbs or 1 tsp dried mixed herbs

1 tsp freshly chopped sage or 1 pinch of dried sage

1 medium egg yolk, lightly beaten

plain flour for coating

vegetable oil for shallow-frying

salt and ground black pepper

mashed potatoes and a green vegetable or grilled bacon and tomatoes to serve

1 Put the minced pork and veal into a large mixing bowl and add the suet, breadcrumbs, lemon zest, nutmeg and herbs. Mix together and season to taste. Add the egg yolk to the mixture and mix well with a fork until all the ingredients are thoroughly combined and bound together.

2 With floured hands, form the mixture into sausage shapes. Coat each sausage in flour, shaking off any excess.

3 Heat a little vegetable oil in a pan and cook the sausages, turning frequently, until evenly browned and cooked through. Serve the sausages with mashed potatoes and a green vegetable as a main meal, or with grilled bacon and tomatoes for breakfast.

Sausage & Mash

Serves 4
Preparation Time
10 minutes,
plus chilling
Cooking Time
50 minutes

Per Serving
643 calories
39g fat
(of which 16g saturates)
56g carbohydrate
2.5g salt

½ tsp vegetable oil
8 good-quality sausages
900g (2lb) Desiree potatoes, cut into chunks
40g (1½oz) butter
1 large leek, thinly sliced
3 tbsp warm milk
1 tbsp wholegrain mustard
4 tbsp red onion marmalade
salt and ground black pepper
steamed carrots and broccoli to serve

1 Heat the oil in a large pan and quickly brown the sausages over a high heat, turning often. Turn the heat down to its lowest setting and leave to cook gently for 30 minutes or until cooked through, turning occasionally. Put the pan to one side.

2 Put the potatoes into a large pan of salted water, cover, bring to the boil, then reduce the heat and simmer for 15–20 minutes until tender. Drain and leave for 2 minutes to steam dry – this will ensure the mash doesn't turn watery.

3 While the potatoes are simmering, melt half the butter in clean pan and fry the leek over a gentle heat, covered, for 25 minutes until softened.

4 Melt the remaining butter in the empty potato pan and add the milk. Add the potatoes and mash until creamy. Stir in the leek and mustard and season. Serve with the sausages, red onion marmalade and steamed carrots and broccoli.

Toad in the Hole

Serves 2

Preparation Time
10 minutes

Cooking Time
25-30 minutes

Per Serving
571 calories
31g fat
(of which 8g saturates)
57g carbohydrate
2.6g salt

125g (4oz) plain flour, sifted
2 large eggs, lightly beaten
150ml (¼ pint) semi-skimmed milk
2 tbsp oil
4 pork sausages
salt and ground black pepper
steamed carrots and broccoli or
green beans to serve

1 Preheat the oven to 220°C (200°C fan oven) mark 7.
Put the flour into a bowl, make a well in the centre
and pour in the eggs and milk. Whisk the batter
thoroughly and season it well with salt and pepper.

2 Put the oil and sausages in a 1 litre (1¾ pint) shallow
ovenproof dish and cook in the oven for 10 minutes,
turning once or twice.

3 Add the batter to the dish and continue to cook for
15-20 minutes until the batter is puffy and a rich
golden colour all over. Serve immediately, with steamed
carrots and broccoli or green beans.

Cumberland Glazed Baked Gammon

Serves 16
Preparation Time
30 minutes
Cooking Time
3½–4¼ hours

Per Serving
406 calories
21g fat
(of which 7g saturates)
4g carbohydrate
6.3g salt

4.5kg (10lb) smoked gammon joint, on the bone
2 celery sticks, roughly chopped
1 onion, quartered
1 carrot, roughly chopped
1 tsp black peppercorns
1 tbsp cloves
75g (3oz) redcurrant sprigs

For the Cumberland glaze
grated zest and juice of ½ lemon and ½ orange
4 tbsp redcurrant jelly
1 tsp Dijon mustard
2 tbsp port
salt and ground black pepper

1 Put the gammon into a large pan. Add the celery, onion, carrot and peppercorns. Cover the meat and vegetables with cold water and bring to the boil. Reduce the heat and simmer, covered, for 2¾–3½ hours, or allowing 15–20 minutes per 450g (1lb) plus 15 minutes. Lift the gammon out of the pan. Preheat the oven to 200°C (180°C fan oven) mark 6.

2 Meanwhile, make the glaze. Heat the lemon and orange zests and juices, redcurrant jelly, mustard and port in a pan to dissolve the jelly. Bring to the boil and bubble for 5 minutes or until syrupy. Season with salt and pepper to taste.

3 Remove the gammon rind and score the fat in a diamond pattern. Put the gammon into a roasting tin, then stud the fat with cloves. Spoon the glaze evenly over the gammon joint.

4 Roast the gammon for 40 minutes, basting the meat with any juices. Add the redcurrant sprigs 10 minutes before the end of the cooking time. Serve the gammon either hot or cold, carved into thin slices with the redcurrant sprigs.

Chicken Kiev

Serves 6
Preparation Time 15 minutes, plus chilling
Cooking Time 45 minutes

Per serving
594 calories
41g fat
(of which 19g saturates)
20g carbohydrate
1.2g salt

175g (6oz) butter, softened
grated zest of ½ lemon
1 tbsp lemon juice
1 tbsp freshly chopped parsley
1 garlic clove, crushed
6 large boneless, skinless chicken breasts
25g (1oz) seasoned flour
1 medium egg, beaten
125g (4oz) fresh breadcrumbs
vegetable oil for deep-frying
salt and ground black pepper
potato wedges and peas to serve

1 Put the butter, lemon zest and juice, parsley, garlic and salt and pepper to taste into a bowl and beat well to combine. (Alternatively, whiz in a food processor.) Form into a roll, cover and chill for at least 1 hour.

2 Put the chicken breasts on a flat surface and, using a meat mallet or rolling pin, pound them to an even thickness. Cut the butter into six pieces and put one piece on the centre of each chicken breast. Roll up, folding the ends in to enclose the butter completely. Secure the rolls with wooden cocktail sticks.

3 Put the seasoned flour, beaten egg and breadcrumbs in three separate flat dishes. Coat each chicken roll with the flour, then turn them in the beaten egg and coat them with breadcrumbs, patting the crumbs firmly on to the chicken.

4 Put the rolls on to a baking sheet, cover lightly with non-stick or greaseproof paper and chill in the fridge for 2 hours or until required, to allow the coating to dry.

5 Heat the oil in a deep-fryer to 160°C (test by frying a small cube of bread; it should brown in 60 seconds). Put two chicken rolls into a frying basket and lower into the oil. Fry for 15 minutes – the chicken is cooked when it is browned and firm when pressed with a fork. Do not pierce.

6 Remove the rolls from the fryer, drain on kitchen paper and keep them warm while you cook the remaining chicken rolls. Remove the cocktail sticks before serving.

7 Serve with potato wedges and peas.

Try Something Different
Spicy Chicken Kiev To make a spicy butter filling, sauté 1 finely chopped shallot with 2 tsp cayenne pepper in 1 tbsp butter until soft but not brown. Cool. Stir in 1 tbsp freshly chopped parsley. Combine with 175g (6oz) softened butter and season. Form into a roll, cover and chill in the fridge for at least 1 hour as step 1, then continue with the recipe.

Saffron Risotto with Lemon Chicken

Serves 4
Preparation Time
20 minutes
Cooking Time
30 minutes

Per Serving
830 calories
44g fat
(of which 15g saturates)
50g carbohydrate
0.9g salt

Gluten Free

zest and juice of 1 lemon
a small handful of fresh parsley
25g (1oz) blanched almonds
1 tbsp dried thyme
1 garlic clove
75ml (2½fl oz) olive oil
450ml (¾ pint) chicken stock
4 boneless chicken breasts, skin on
50g (2oz) butter
225g (8oz) onions, finely chopped
a small pinch of saffron threads
225g (8oz) arborio rice
125ml (4fl oz) white wine
50g (2oz) freshly grated Parmesan
salt and ground black pepper
fresh thyme sprigs and lemon wedges to garnish

1 Preheat the oven to 200°C (180°C fan oven) mark 6. Whiz the lemon zest, parsley, almonds, thyme and garlic in a food processor for a few seconds, then slowly add the oil and whiz until combined. Season with salt and pepper. Heat the stock in a pan to a steady low simmer.

2 Spread the lemon and herb mixture under the skin of the chicken. Put the chicken into a roasting tin, brush with 25g (1oz) melted butter and pour the lemon juice over it. Cook in the oven for 25 minutes, basting occasionally.

3 Heat the remaining butter in a pan. Add the onions and fry until soft. Stir in the saffron and rice. Add the wine to the rice. Gradually add the hot stock, a ladleful at a time, stirring with each addition and allowing it to be absorbed before adding more. This will take about 25 minutes. Take the pan off the heat and stir in the Parmesan. Serve with the chicken, pouring any juices from the roasting tin over it. Garnish with thyme sprigs and lemon wedges.

Chicken Tikka Masala

Serves 4

Preparation Time

15 minutes

Cooking Time

30 minutes

Per Serving

297 calories

17g fat

(of which 4g saturates)

4g carbohydrate

0.6g salt

Gluten Free Dairy Free

2 tbsp vegetable oil

1 onion, finely sliced

2 garlic cloves, crushed

6 boneless, skinless chicken thighs, cut into strips

2 tbsp tikka masala curry paste

200g can chopped tomatoes

450ml (¾ pint) hot vegetable stock

225g (8oz) baby spinach leaves

fresh coriander leaves to garnish

plain boiled rice, mango chutney and poppadoms to serve

1 Heat the oil in a large pan, add the onion and fry over a medium heat for 5–7 minutes until golden. Add the garlic and chicken and stir-fry for about 5 minutes or until golden.

2 Stir in the curry paste, then add the tomatoes and hot stock. Bring to the boil, then reduce the heat, cover the pan and simmer over a low heat for 15 minutes or until the chicken is cooked through.

3 Add the spinach to the curry, stir and cook until the leaves have just wilted. Garnish with coriander and serve with plain boiled rice, mango chutney and poppadoms.

Chicken Fajitas

Serves 4
Preparation Time
10 minutes
Cooking Time
20 minutes

Per Serving
651 calories
23g fat
(of which 8g saturates)
63g carbohydrate
1.6g salt

700g (1½lb) boneless, skinless chicken breasts,
cut into chunky strips
2 tbsp fajita seasoning
1 tbsp sunflower oil
1 red pepper, seeded and sliced
360g jar fajita sauce
1 bunch of spring onions, halved
8 large flour tortillas
150g (5oz) tomato salsa
125g (4oz) guacamole dip
150ml (¼ pint) soured cream

1 Put the chicken breasts into a shallow dish and toss together with the fajita seasoning. Heat the oil in a large non-stick frying pan, add the chicken and cook for 5 minutes or until golden brown and tender.

2 Add the red pepper and cook for 2 minutes. Pour in the fajita sauce and bring to the boil, then reduce the heat and simmer for 5 minutes or until thoroughly heated. Add a splash of boiling water if the sauce becomes too thick. Stir in the spring onions and cook for 2 minutes.

3 Meanwhile, warm the tortillas in a microwave on full power for 45 seconds, or wrap in foil and warm in a preheated oven at 180°C (160°C fan oven) mark 4 for 10 minutes.

4 Transfer the chicken to a serving dish and take to the table, along with the tortillas, salsa, guacamole and soured cream. Let everyone help themselves.

Chicken & Bacon Pie

Serves 4
Preparation Time
30 minutes,
plus cooling
Cooking Time
about 55 minutes

Per Serving
554 calories
34g fat
(of which 6g saturates)
24g carbohydrate
1.3g salt

1 tbsp olive oil
4 skinless, boneless chicken breasts, cut into
2.5cm (1in) cubes
1 medium onion, sliced
1 carrot, roughly chopped
50g (2oz) smoked streaky bacon, rind removed
and chopped
1 tbsp plain flour, plus extra to dust
200ml (7fl oz) chicken stock
100ml (3½fl oz) double cream
25g (1oz) frozen peas
1½ tsp wholegrain mustard
1 tbsp freshly chopped tarragon
175g (6oz) puff pastry, thawed if frozen
1 medium egg, beaten
salt and ground black pepper

1 Heat half the oil in a large pan, then brown the chicken in batches. Remove from the pan and put to one side. Add the remaining oil and fry the onion and carrot for 10 minutes. Add the bacon and cook for 3 minutes.

2 Stir in the flour and cook for 1 minute. Gradually add the stock, stirring well. Add the cream and return the chicken and any juices to the pan. Simmer for 5 minutes or until the chicken is cooked.

3 Add the peas, mustard and tarragon, then check the seasoning. Leave to cool a little.

4 Preheat the oven to 200°C (180°C fan oven) mark 6. Put a pie funnel, if you have one, in the centre of a 1 litre (1¾ pint) pie dish or ovenproof casserole and tip in the filling. Roll out the pastry on a lightly floured surface to make a lid and cut a slit for the pie funnel. Brush the edge of the pastry all round with the egg, then lay the pastry, brushed side down, over the dish, press to seal and trim with a sharp knife. Brush with beaten egg and cook in the oven for 25–30 minutes until golden.

Get Ahead
Assemble the pie, then cover and chill for up to two days. To use, brush with beaten egg and complete the recipe.

Classic Roast Chicken

Serves 5	1.4kg (3lb) chicken
Preparation Time	2 garlic cloves
30 minutes	1 onion, cut into wedges
Cooking Time	2 tsp sea salt
about 1 hour	2 tsp ground black pepper
20 minutes,	4 fresh flat-leafed parsley sprigs
plus resting	4 fresh tarragon sprigs
	2 bay leaves
Per Serving	50g (2oz) butter,
682 calories	cut into cubes
49g fat	salt and ground black pepper
(of which 21g saturates)	
17g carbohydrate	
1g salt	

For the stuffing
40g (1½oz) butter
1 small onion, chopped
1 garlic clove, crushed
75g (3oz) fresh white breadcrumbs
finely grated zest and juice of 1 small lemon,
halves reserved for the chicken
2 tbsp each freshly chopped flat-leafed
parsley and tarragon
1 medium egg yolk

For the gravy
200ml (7fl oz) white wine
1 tbsp Dijon mustard
450ml (¾ pint) hot chicken stock
25g (1oz) butter, mixed with 25g (1oz) plain
flour (beurre manié, see Cook's Tip)

1 To make the stuffing, melt the butter in a pan, add the onion and garlic and fry for 5–10 minutes until soft. Cool, then add the remaining ingredients, stirring in the egg yolk last. Season well.

2 Preheat the oven to 190°C (170°C fan oven) mark 5. Put the chicken on a board, breast upwards, then put the garlic, onion, reserved lemon halves and half the salt, pepper and herb sprigs into the body cavity.

3 Lift the loose skin at the neck and fill the cavity with stuffing. Turn the bird on to its breast and pull the neck flap over the opening to cover the stuffing. Rest the wing tips across it and truss the chicken (see step 4, page 61). Weigh the stuffed bird to calculate the cooking time and allow 20 minutes per 450g (1lb), plus an extra 20 minutes.

4 Put the chicken on a rack in a roasting tin. Season with the remaining salt and pepper, then top with the remaining herbs and the bay leaves. Dot with the butter and roast, basting halfway through, until cooked and the juices run clear when the thickest part of the thigh is pierced with a skewer.

5 Put the chicken on a serving dish, cover with foil and leave to rest while you make the gravy. Pour off all but about 3 tbsp fat from the tin, put the tin over a high heat, add the wine and boil for 2 minutes. Add the mustard and hot stock and bring back to the boil. Gradually whisk in knobs of the butter mixture until smooth, then season with salt and pepper. Carve the chicken and serve with the stuffing and gravy.

Cook's Tip

Beurre Manié A beurre manié is a mixture of equal parts of softened butter and flour that has been kneaded together to form a paste. It is used to thicken sauces and stews and is whisked in towards the end of cooking, then boiled briefly to allow it to thicken.

Roast Turkey with Parsley, Sage & Thyme

Serves 16	6.3kg (14lb) turkey
Preparation Time	2 small red onions, cut into wedges
40 minutes, plus	2 lemons, cut into wedges
cooling and chilling	6 whole garlic cloves
Cooking Time	8 fresh thyme sprigs
3¾ hours	8 fresh sage leaves
	8 fresh flat-leafed parsley sprigs
Per Serving	250ml (9fl oz) olive oil
280 calories	roast vegetables to serve
10g fat	
(of which 2g saturates)	**For the seasoning**
11g carbohydrate	1 tbsp whole pink peppercorns
2.2g salt	2 tsp sea salt
	2 tbsp paprika
	2 tbsp celery salt

For the stuffing
4 tbsp olive oil
2 large onions, finely chopped
4 garlic cloves, crushed
150g (5oz) fresh white breadcrumbs
75g (3oz) medium cornmeal or polenta
100g (3½oz) hazelnuts, toasted and chopped
finely grated zest of 2 lemons and juice
of 1 lemon
4 tbsp freshly chopped flat-leafed parsley
4 tbsp freshly chopped sage
2 medium eggs, lightly beaten
salt and ground black pepper

1 To make the stuffing, heat the oil in a pan. Add the onions and garlic and fry gently for 10 minutes to soften but not brown. Tip into a bowl to cool. Meanwhile, put the breadcrumbs, cornmeal or polenta, hazelnuts, lemon zest, parsley, sage and eggs into a large bowl and squeeze in the lemon juice. Add the cooled onion and garlic and season. Stir to bind together, and leave to cool.

2 To make the seasoning, put the peppercorns, sea salt, paprika and celery salt into a mortar and pound with a pestle to crush, or whiz in a mini processor. Stand the turkey upright on a board, with the parson's nose (the rear end) facing upwards. Sprinkle the inside cavity with 1 tbsp of the peppercorn seasoning, then pack the cavity with half the onions and lemon wedges, garlic cloves, thyme and sage and all the parsley sprigs.

3 Sit the turkey with the parson's nose facing away from you. Lift up the loose skin at the neck end with one hand and, using the other, fill the cavity with handfuls of cold stuffing. Turn the turkey over on to its breast, then lift the neck flap up and over the stuffing to cover and bring the wing tips round on top.

4 Thread a trussing needle with 2m (6ft) fine string and sew the neck flap to the turkey. Push the skewer firmly through the wings, twist the string around the ends and pull to tighten so that both wings are snug against the breast. Turn the turkey over, tuck in the parson's nose, cross the legs together, then bring the string up and over the legs and wrap around tightly, finishing with a double knot to secure. Cut off any excess.

5 Pour the oil into a large roasting tin. Immerse a piece of muslin, about 60cm (24in) long, in it to coat completely, then stretch it out, with the edges overhanging the tin. Sit the turkey on top and sprinkle with the remaining peppercorn seasoning. Scatter over the remaining thyme and sage, then arrange the remaining lemon and onion wedges and the garlic cloves around the bird. Bring the muslin up and over the turkey to wrap completely, then turn it over so that it's breast side down in the tin. Over-wrap with clingfilm and leave to chill overnight in the bottom of the fridge. Remember to take it out 30 minutes before cooking so that it has time to come to room temperature.

6 Remove the muslin and keep the turkey breast side down. Preheat the oven to 180°C (160°C fan oven) mark 4. Roast the turkey for about 3¾ hours, basting occasionally to keep the flesh moist. Turn the turkey over after cooking for 1 hour 50 minutes. Check the turkey is cooked by piercing the thickest part of the thigh with a skewer – the juices should run clear. Serve with vegetables.

Roast Leg of Lamb with Rosemary

Serves 8
Preparation Time
15 minutes
Cooking Time
1½ hours,
plus resting

Per Serving
601 calories
39g fat
(of which 17g saturates)
1g carbohydrate
1.3g salt

2.5kg (5½lb) leg of lamb
4 rosemary sprigs
½ tbsp oil
4 garlic cloves, cut into slivers
4 anchovy fillets, roughly chopped
4 oregano sprigs
1 large onion, thickly sliced
1 lemon, cut into 6 wedges
salt and ground black pepper
carrots and green beans to serve

1 Take the lamb out of the fridge 1 hour before roasting. Pat the skin dry with kitchen paper.

2 Preheat the oven to 220°C (200°C fan oven) mark 7. Cut the rosemary into smaller sprigs. Rub the oil over the lamb. Cut small slits all over the meat, then insert the garlic slivers, rosemary sprigs, anchovy pieces and the leaves from two oregano sprigs into the gaps. Season well.

3 Put the onion slices into the bottom of a roasting tin just large enough to hold the lamb. Top with the remaining oregano, then put in the meat, fat side up (the onions must be covered to prevent them burning). Tuck lemon wedges around the meat.

4 Put the lamb into the oven and reduce the oven temperature to 190°C (170°C fan oven) mark 5. Roast for 15 minutes per 450lb (1lb) for pink meat, or longer if you like it more cooked.

5 Transfer the lamb to a board, cover with foil and leave to rest for 30 minutes before carving. Carefully pour (or skim) off the fat from a corner of the roasting tin, leaving the sediment behind. Put the tin on the hob over a medium heat and pour in 300–450ml (½–¾ pint) vegetable water (or meat stock). Stir thoroughly, scraping up the sediment, and boil steadily until the gravy is a rich brown colour. Serve the lamb with the gravy and carrots and green beans.

Get Ahead
Prepare the lamb to the end of step 3 up to 2 hours ahead. To use, complete the recipe.

Cook's Tip
The lamb is served pink here, but allow an extra 20–30 minutes if you prefer your meat more cooked.

Minted Lamb Burgers with Cucumber

Serves 4
Preparation Time
15 minutes
Cooking Time
30 minutes

Per Serving
374 calories
17g fat
(of which 7g saturates)
28g carbohydrate
1.6g salt

450g (1lb) minced lamb
1 small onion, finely chopped
125g (4oz) fresh breadcrumbs
finely grated zest of ½ lemon
1 medium egg, beaten
3 tbsp freshly chopped mint
2 tbsp plain flour
½ cucumber, cut into 5cm (2in) long wedges
6 spring onions, trimmed and cut into
1cm (½in) pieces
200ml (7fl oz) lamb or chicken stock
1 tbsp dry sherry
salt and ground black pepper
boiled new potatoes to serve

1 Mix the lamb, onion, breadcrumbs and lemon zest with the egg and 1 tbsp of the chopped mint. Season. Shape into eight burgers with floured hands, then completely coat in the flour.

2 Dry-fry the burgers in a large, heavy-based non-stick frying pan for about 6 minutes, until lightly browned, turning once. Add the cucumber and spring onions.

3 Pour in the stock and sherry, then add the remaining mint and salt and pepper to taste. Bring to the boil, cover, reduce the heat and simmer gently for about 20 minutes or until the meat is tender. Skim off any excess fat before serving and taste and adjust the seasoning. Serve with boiled new potatoes.

Lamb Chops with Crispy Garlic Potatoes

Serves 4
Preparation Time
10 minutes
Cooking Time
20 minutes

Per serving
835 calories
45g fat
(of which 19g saturates)
22g carbohydrate
0.7g salt

2 tbsp mint sauce
8 small lamb chops
3 medium potatoes, cut into 5mm (¼in) slices
2 tbsp Garlic-infused Olive Oil (see Cook's Tip)
1 tbsp olive oil
salt and ground black pepper
steamed green beans to serve

1 Spread the mint sauce over the lamb chops and leave to marinate while you prepare the potatoes.

2 Boil the potatoes in a pan of lightly salted water for 2 minutes or until just starting to soften. Drain, tip back into the pan and season, then add the garlic oil and toss to combine.

3 Meanwhile, heat the olive oil in a large frying pan and fry the chops for 4–5 minutes on each side until just cooked, adding a splash of boiling water to the pan to make a sauce. Remove the chops and sauce from the pan and keep warm.

4 Add the potatoes to the pan. Fry over a medium heat for 10–12 minutes until crisp and golden. Divide the potatoes, chops and sauce among four warmed plates and serve with green beans.

Cook's Tip
Garlic-infused Olive Oil Gently heat 2 tbsp olive oil with a peeled sliced garlic clove for 5 minutes and use immediately. Do not store.

Irish Stew

Serves 4
Preparation Time
15 minutes
Cooking Time
about 2¼ hours

Per Serving
419 calories
20g fat
(of which 9g saturates)
24g carbohydrate
0.6g salt

700g (1½lb) middle neck lamb cutlets,
fat trimmed
2 onions, thinly sliced
450g (1lb) potatoes, peeled and thinly sliced
1 tbsp freshly chopped flat-leafed parsley,
plus extra to garnish
1 tbsp dried thyme
300ml (½ pint) lamb stock
salt and ground black pepper

1 Preheat the oven to 170°C (150°C fan oven) mark 3.
Layer the meat, onions and potatoes in a deep
casserole dish, sprinkling some herbs and seasoning
between each layer. Finish with a layer of potato,
overlapping the slices neatly.

2 Pour the stock over the potatoes, then cover with
greaseproof paper and a lid. Cook for about 2 hours
or until the meat is tender.

3 Preheat the grill. Take the lid off the casserole and
remove the paper. Put under the grill and brown
the top of the potatoes. Sprinkle with chopped parsley
and serve immediately.

Shepherd's Pie

Serves 4
Preparation Time
20 minutes
Cooking Time
about 1 hour

Per Serving
513 calories
27g fat
(of which 11g saturates)
44g carbohydrate
0.6g salt

2 tbsp sunflower oil
450g (1lb) minced lamb
1 large onion, chopped
50g (2oz) mushrooms, sliced
2 carrots, chopped
2 tbsp plain flour
1 tbsp tomato purée
1 bay leaf (optional)
300ml (½ pint) lamb or vegetable stock
(see Cook's Tip)
700g (1½lb) potatoes, peeled and cut into
large chunks
25g (1oz) butter
60ml (2¼fl oz) milk
50g (2oz) Cheddar cheese, crumbled (optional)
salt and ground black pepper
green vegetables to serve

1 Heat half the oil in a large pan and brown the mince over a medium to high heat – do this in batches, otherwise the meat will steam rather than fry. Remove with a slotted spoon on to a plate.

2 Turn the heat to low and add the remaining oil. Gently fry the onion, mushrooms and carrots for 10 minutes or until softened. Stir in the flour and tomato purée and cook for 1 minute. Return the meat to the pan and add the bay leaf, if you like. Pour in the stock and bring to the boil, then cover and simmer on a low heat for 25 minutes.

3 Preheat the oven to 200°C (180°C fan oven) mark 6. Cook the potatoes in lightly salted boiling water for 20 minutes or until tender. Drain and leave to stand in the colander for 2 minutes to steam dry. Melt the butter and milk in the potato pan and add the cooked potatoes. Mash until smooth.

4 Spoon the lamb mixture into a 1.7 litre (3 pint) casserole dish. Remove the bay leaf and check the seasoning. Cover with the mashed potato and sprinkle the cheese over, if you like. Bake for 15–20 minutes until bubbling and golden. Serve immediately with green vegetables.

Cook's Tip
You can use 1 lamb or vegetable stock cube dissolved in 300ml (½ pint) boiling water.

Cottage Pie

Serves 4
Preparation Time
15 minutes
Cooking Time
about 1 hour

Per serving
581 calories
28g fat
(of which 12g saturates)
55g carbohydrate
1.8g salt

1 tbsp olive oil
1 onion, peeled and finely chopped
2 garlic cloves, peeled and crushed
450g (1lb) minced beef
1 tbsp plain flour
450ml (¾ pint) beef stock
2 tbsp Worcestershire sauce
1 medium carrot, peeled and diced
125g (4oz) button mushrooms, sliced
1kg (2¼lb) potatoes, roughly chopped
25g (1oz) butter
75ml (3fl oz) milk
salt and ground black pepper

1 Heat the oil in a large pan, add the onion and fry over a medium heat for 15 minutes until softened and golden, stirring occasionally. Add the garlic and cook for 1 minute.

2 Preheat the oven to 200°C (180°C fan oven) mark 6. Add the beef to the onion and garlic and, as it browns, use a wooden spoon to break up the pieces. Once it's brown, stir in the flour. Stir in the stock to the browned mince, cover the pan with a lid and bring to the boil. Add the Worcestershire sauce, carrot and mushrooms and season well with salt and pepper. Reduce the heat, cover and cook for 15 minutes.

3 Meanwhile, put the potatoes into a large pan of salted water. Bring to the boil and cook for about 20–25 minutes until very soft. Drain and put back into the pan over a low heat to dry off. Mash until smooth, and then beat in the butter and milk. Season with salt and pepper to taste.

4 Spoon the sauce into a 1.7 litre (3 pint) ovenproof dish, cover with the mashed potato, then cook in the oven for 20–25 minutes or until piping hot and the topping is golden brown.

Try Something Different
To make individual pies, use four 450ml (¾ pint) shallow ovenproof dishes.

Beef Stroganoff

Serves 4	700g (1½lb) rump or fillet steak, trimmed
Preparation Time	50g (2oz) unsalted butter or 4 tbsp olive oil
10 minutes	1 onion, thinly sliced
Cooking Time	225g (8oz) brown-cap mushrooms, sliced
about 20 minutes	3 tbsp brandy
	1 tsp French mustard
Per serving	200ml (7fl oz) crème fraîche
750 calories	100ml (3½fl oz) double cream
60g fat	3 tbsp freshly chopped flat-leafed parsley
(of which 35g saturates)	salt and ground black pepper
3g carbohydrate	rice or noodles to serve
0.5g salt	

1 Cut the steak into strips about 5mm (¼in) wide and 5cm (2in) long.

2 Heat half the butter or oil in a large heavy frying pan over a medium heat. Add the onion and cook gently for 10 minutes or until soft and golden. Remove with a slotted spoon and put to one side. Add the mushrooms to the pan and cook, stirring, for 2–3 minutes until golden brown; remove and put to one side.

3 Increase the heat and add the remaining butter or oil to the pan. Quickly fry the meat, in two or three batches, for 2–3 minutes, stirring constantly to ensure even browning. Remove from the pan. Add the brandy to the pan and allow it to bubble to reduce.

4 Put all the meat, onion and mushrooms back into the pan. Reduce the heat and stir in the mustard, crème fraîche and cream. Heat through, stir in most of the parsley and season with salt and pepper. Serve with rice or noodles, with the remaining chopped parsley scattered over the top.

Freezing Tip
To freeze, complete the recipe, transfer to a freezerproof container, cool, label and freeze for up to three months.
To use, thaw overnight in the fridge. Put in a pan, cover and bring to the boil; reduce the heat to low and simmer until piping hot.

Meat Loaf

Serves 4
Preparation Time
10 minutes
Cooking Time
1 hour 40 minutes

Per serving
406 calories
26g fat
(of which 12g saturates)
17g carbohydrate
1.4g salt

25g (1oz) butter, plus extra to grease
1 onion, finely chopped
1 tsp paprika
450g (1lb) minced beef
50g (2oz) fresh breadcrumbs
3 tbsp natural wheatgerm
1 garlic clove, crushed
1 tbsp freshly chopped herbs or 1 tsp dried mixed
herbs, plus fresh herbs to garnish
4 tbsp tomato purée
1 medium egg, beaten
salt and ground black pepper
fresh tomato sauce to serve (see Cook's Tip page 23)

1 Preheat the oven to 180°C (160°C fan oven) mark 4.
Grease and base line a 450g (1lb), capacity 900ml
(1½ pint), loaf tin.

2 Melt the butter in a frying pan, add the onion and
cook until softened. Add the paprika and cook for
1 minute, stirring, then turn the mixture into a large bowl.

3 Add all the remaining ingredients and stir
thoroughly until evenly mixed. Spoon the mixture
into the loaf tin, level the surface and cover tightly
with foil.

4 Stand the loaf tin in a roasting tin and pour in
water to a depth of 2.5cm (1in). Cook in the oven
for 1½ hours. Turn out and serve with the sauce.

Hamburgers

Serves 6
Preparation Time
20 minutes,
plus chilling
Cooking Time
10 minutes

Per serving
645 calories
45g fat
(of which 17g saturates)
19g carbohydrate
2.3g salt

1kg (2¼lb) extra-lean minced beef
2 tsp salt
2 tbsp steak seasoning
sunflower oil to brush
6 large soft rolls, halved
6 thin-cut slices havarti or raclette cheese
4 small cocktail gherkins, sliced lengthways
6 tbsp mustard mayonnaise
6 lettuce leaves, such as frisée
4 large vine-ripened tomatoes, sliced thickly
2 large shallots, sliced into thin rings
ground black pepper

1 Put the minced beef into a large bowl and add the salt, steak seasoning and plenty of pepper. Use your hands to mix the ingredients together thoroughly. Lightly oil the inside of six 10cm (4in) rosti rings and put on a foil-lined baking sheet. Press the meat firmly into the rings, or use your hands to shape the mixture into six even-sized patties. Cover with clingfilm and chill for at least 1 hour.

2 Heat a large griddle pan until it's really hot. Put the rolls, cut sides down, on the griddle and toast.

3 Lightly oil the griddle, ease the burgers out of the moulds and brush with oil. Griddle over a medium heat for about 3 minutes, then turn the burgers over carefully. Put a slice of cheese and a few slices of gherkin on top of each and cook for another 3 minutes. While the burgers are cooking, spread the mustard mayonnaise on the toasted side of the rolls. Add the lettuce, tomatoes and shallots. Put the burgers on top and sandwich with the other half-rolls.

Try Something Different
For a more sophisticated burger, replace the cheese and gherkins with thick slices of ripe avocado and use a generous handful of fresh rocket instead of the lettuce.

Chilli Con Carne

Serves 4
Preparation Time
5 minutes
Cooking Time
about 1 hour

Per serving
408 calories
19g fat
(of which 7g saturates)
28g carbohydrate
1.1g salt

2 tbsp olive oil
450g (1lb) minced beef
1 large onion, finely chopped
1 tsp each hot chilli powder and ground cumin
3 tbsp tomato purée
300ml (½ pint) hot vegetable stock
400g can chopped tomatoes with garlic
(see Cook's Tips)
25g (1oz) dark chocolate (see Cook's Tips)
400g can red kidney beans, drained and rinsed
2 × 20g packs coriander, chopped
salt and ground black pepper
guacamole, salsa, soured cream, grated cheese,
tortilla chips and pickled chillies to serve

1 Heat 1 tbsp oil in a large non-stick pan and fry the beef for 10 minutes or until well browned, stirring to break up any lumps. Remove from the pan with a slotted spoon and set aside.

2 Add the remaining oil to the pan, then fry the onion, stirring, for 10 minutes or until soft and golden.

3 Add the spices and fry for 1 minute, then return the beef to the pan. Add the tomato purée, hot stock and tomatoes. Bring to the boil, then reduce to a simmer. Continue to bubble gently, uncovered, for 35–40 minutes, or until the sauce is well reduced and the mixture is quite thick.

4 Stir in the chocolate, kidney beans and coriander, season with salt and pepper, then simmer for 5 minutes.

5 Serve with guacamole, salsa, soured cream, grated cheese, tortilla chips and pickled chillies.

Cook's Tips
Instead of a can of tomatoes with garlic, use a can of chopped tomatoes and 1 crushed garlic clove.
Adding a little dark chocolate to chilli con carne brings out the flavours of this tasty dish.

Roast Rib of Beef

Serves 8

Preparation Time

5 minutes

Cooking Time

2½ hours, plus resting

Per serving

807 calories

53g fat

(of which 24g saturates)

2g carbohydrate

0.5g salt

2-bone rib of beef, about 2.5–2.7kg (5½–6lb)
1 tbsp plain flour
1 tbsp mustard powder
150ml (¼ pint) red wine
600ml (1 pint) beef stock
600ml (1 pint) water
salt and ground black pepper
thyme sprigs to garnish
Yorkshire Puddings (see page 77), roasted root
vegetables and a green vegetable to serve

1 Preheat the oven to 230°C (210°C fan oven) mark 8. Put the beef, fat side up, in a roasting tin just large enough to hold the joint. Mix the flour and mustard together in a small bowl and season with salt and pepper, then rub the mixture over the beef. Roast in the centre of the oven for 30 minutes.

2 Move the beef to a lower shelf, near the bottom of the oven. Reduce the oven temperature to 220°C (200°C fan oven) mark 7 and continue to roast the beef for a further 2 hours, basting occasionally.

3 Put the beef on a carving dish, cover loosely with foil and leave to rest while you make the gravy. Skim off most of the fat from the roasting tin. Put the roasting tin on the hob, pour in the wine and boil vigorously until very syrupy. Pour in the stock and, again, boil until syrupy. Add the vegetable water and boil until syrupy. There should be about 450ml (¾ pint) gravy. Taste and adjust the seasoning.

4 Remove the rib bone and carve the beef. Garnish with thyme and serve with the gravy and Yorkshire puddings and roasted vegetables.

Cook's Tip
Buy the best quality meat you can afford. The beef should be a dark red colour, not bright red, and have a good marbling of fat.

Classic Roast Beef with Yorkshire Puddings

Serves 8
Preparation Time
20 minutes
Cooking Time
about 1½ hours,
plus resting

Per Serving
510 calories
24g fat
(of which 9g saturates)
16g carbohydrate
0.5g salt

1 boned and rolled rib, sirloin, rump or
topside of beef, about 1.8kg (4lb)
1 tbsp plain flour
1 tbsp mustard powder
salt and ground black pepper
fresh thyme sprigs to garnish
vegetables to serve

For the Yorkshire pudding
125g (4oz) plain flour
½ tsp salt
300ml (½ pint) milk
2 medium eggs

For the gravy
150ml (¼ pint) red wine
600ml (1 pint) beef stock

1 Preheat the oven to 230°C (210°C fan oven) mark 8. Put the beef into a roasting tin, thickest part of the fat uppermost. Mix the flour with the mustard powder and salt and pepper. Rub the mixture over the beef. Roast the beef in the centre of the oven for 30 minutes.

2 Baste the beef and reduce the oven temperature to 190°C (170°C fan oven) mark 5. Cook for a further 1 hour, basting occasionally.

3 Meanwhile, prepare the Yorkshire pudding batter. Sift the flour and salt into a bowl. Mix in half the milk, then add the eggs and season with pepper. Beat until smooth, then whisk in the remaining milk.

4 Put the beef on a warmed carving dish, cover loosely with foil and leave to rest in a warm place. Increase the oven temperature to 220°C (200°C fan oven) mark 7.

5 Pour off about 3 tbsp fat from the roasting tin and use to grease 8–12 individual Yorkshire pudding tins. Heat in the oven for 5 minutes or until the fat is almost smoking. Pour the Yorkshire batter into the tins. Bake for 15–20 minutes until well risen, golden and crisp.

6 Meanwhile, make the gravy. Skim off any remaining fat from the roasting tin. Put the tin on the hob, add the wine and boil until syrupy. Pour in the stock and, again, boil until syrupy – there should be about 450ml (¾ pint) gravy. Taste and adjust the seasoning.

7 Carve the beef into slices. Garnish with thyme and serve with the gravy, Yorkshire puddings and vegetables of your choice.

Chilli Steak & Corn on the Cob

Serves 4
Preparation Time
5 minutes
Cooking Time
15 minutes

Per Serving
564 calories
31g fat
(of which 14g saturates)
33g carbohydrate
1.4g salt

Gluten Free

50g (2oz) butter, softened
1 large red chilli, seeded and finely chopped
1 garlic clove, crushed
25g (1oz) freshly grated Parmesan
1 tbsp finely chopped fresh basil
4 corn on the cob, each cut into three pieces
1 tbsp olive oil
4 sirloin steaks, about 150g (5oz) each
mixed green salad to serve

1 Put the butter into a bowl and beat with a wooden spoon. Add the chilli, garlic, Parmesan and basil and mix everything together. Cover and chill to firm up.

2 Meanwhile, bring a large pan of water to the boil. Add the corn, cover to bring back to the boil, then reduce the heat and simmer, half-covered, for about 10 minutes or until tender. Drain well.

3 Heat the oil in a large frying pan or griddle over a medium heat. Cook the steaks for 2–3 minutes on each side for medium-rare, 3–4 minutes for medium.

4 Divide the corn and steaks among four warmed plates and top with the chilled butter. Serve immediately, with a mixed green salad.

Bread & Butter Pudding

Serves 4
Preparation Time
10 minutes,
plus soaking
Cooking Time
30-40 minutes

Per Serving
450 calories
13g fat
(5g saturates)
70g carbohydrate
1.1g salt

Vegetarian

50g (2oz) butter, softened, plus extra to grease
275g (10oz) white farmhouse bread, cut into 1cm
(½in) slices, crusts removed
50g (2oz) raisins or sultanas
3 medium eggs
450ml (¾ pint) milk
3 tbsp golden icing sugar, plus extra to dust

1 Lightly butter four 300ml (½ pint) gratin dishes or
one 1.1 litre (2 pint) ovenproof dish. Butter the bread,
then cut into triangles. Arrange the bread in the dish(es)
and sprinkle with the raisins or sultanas.

2 Beat the eggs, milk and sugar in a bowl. Pour
the mixture over the bread and leave to soak for
10 minutes. Preheat the oven to 180°C (160°C fan oven)
mark 4.

3 Put the pudding(s) in the oven and bake for 30-40
minutes. Dust with icing sugar to serve.

Jam Roly-poly

Serves 4
Preparation Time
25 minutes
Cooking Time
1 hour

Per Serving
449 calories
22g fat
(of which 13g saturates)
62g carbohydrate
0.7g salt

butter to grease
6 tbsp jam
a little milk
vanilla custard to serve

For the suet crust pastry
175g (6oz) self-raising flour, plus extra to dust
¼ tsp salt
100g (3½oz) shredded suet

1 Preheat the oven to 180°C (160°C fan oven) mark 4. Grease a piece of foil 23 × 33cm (9 × 13in).

2 To make the pastry, sift the flour and salt into a bowl, added the shredded suet and stir to mix. Using a round-bladed knife, mix in enough cold water to make a soft dough – you will need about 100ml (3½fl oz). If the dough seems too dry, add a little extra liquid. Knead very lightly until smooth.

3 Roll out the suet crust pastry on a lightly floured surface to a rectangle about 23 × 28cm (9 × 11in). Spread the jam on the pastry, leaving 5mm (¼in) clear along each edge. Brush the edges with milk and roll up the pastry evenly, starting from one short side.

4 Put the roll on the greased foil and wrap the foil around it loosely, to allow for expansion, but seal the edges well. Put a rack in a roasting tin. Fill with 2.5cm (1in) boiling water, making sure it does not come higher than the rack. Put the foil-covered roll on the rack. Cover the whole tray tightly with foil to make sure no steam escapes. Steam for 1 hour. Remove from the foil and serve with custard.

Eton Mess

Serves 6
Preparation Time
10 minutes

Per Serving
198 calories
5g fat
(of which 3g saturates)
33g carbohydrate
0.1g salt

Vegetarian

200g (7oz) fromage frais, chilled
200g (7oz) low-fat Greek yogurt, chilled
1 tbsp golden caster sugar
2 tbsp strawberry liqueur
6 meringues, roughly crushed
350g (12oz) strawberries, hulled and halved

1 Put the fromage frais and yogurt into a large bowl
and stir to combine.

2 Add the sugar, strawberry liqueur, meringues and
strawberries. Mix together gently and divide among
six dishes.

Try Something Different
Caribbean Crush Replace the sugar and liqueur with
dulce de leche toffee sauce and the strawberries with
sliced bananas.

Classic Apple Pie

Serves 6

Preparation Time
20 minutes, plus chilling

Cooking Time
35-40 minutes

Per serving
268 calories
11g fat
(of which 4g saturates)
43g carbohydrate
0.4g salt

Vegetarian

Pastry
225g (8oz) plain flour, plus extra to dust
pinch of salt
100g (3½oz) chilled butter
1 large egg

For the filling
900g (2lb) cooking apples, peeled, cored and sliced
50g (2oz) caster sugar, plus extra to sprinkle
cream to serve

1. To make the pastry, put the flour and salt into a bowl. Rub the fat into the flour until the mixture resembles fine breadcrumbs. Add the egg, stirring with a round-bladed knife until the ingredients begin to stick together in large lumps. With one hand collect the mixture together and knead lightly for a few seconds to give a firm, smooth dough. Wrap in clingfilm and leave to rest in the fridge for 30 minutes.

2. Preheat the oven to 190°C (170°C fan oven) mark 5. Layer the apples and sugar in a 1.1 litre (2 pint) pie dish. Sprinkle with 1 tbsp water.

3. Roll out the pastry on a lightly floured surface to a round 2.5cm (1in) larger than the pie dish. Cut off a strip the width of the rim of the dish, dampen the rim of the dish and press on the strip. Dampen the pastry strip and cover with the pastry circle, pressing the edges together well. Decorate the edge of the pastry and make a slit in the centre to allow steam to escape.

4. Bake for 35-40 minutes until the pastry is lightly browned. Sprinkle with caster sugar before serving with cream.

Cook's Tip
Apple pie is also great served cold, with a scoop of vanilla ice cream.

Spotted Dick

Serves 4
Preparation Time
20 minutes
Cooking Time
2 hours

Per Serving
502 calories
18g fat
(of which 10g saturates)
84g carbohydrate
0.8g salt

125g (4oz) fresh breadcrumbs
75g (3oz) self-raising flour, plus extra to dust
75g (3oz) shredded suet
50g (2oz) caster sugar
175g (6oz) currants
finely grated zest of 1 lemon
5 tbsp milk
vanilla custard to serve

1 Half-fill a preserving pan or large pan with water and put on to boil.

2 Put the breadcrumbs, flour, suet, sugar, currants and grated lemon zest into a bowl and stir well until thoroughly mixed.

3 Pour in the milk and stir until well blended. Using one hand, bring the ingredients together to form a soft, slightly sticky dough.

4 Turn the dough out on to a floured surface and knead gently until just smooth. Shape into a neat roll about 15cm (6in) in length.

5 Make a 5cm (2in) pleat across a clean teatowel or pudding cloth. (Or pleat together sheets of greased greaseproof paper and strong foil.) Encase the roll in the cloth (or foil), pleating the open edges tightly together.

6 Tie the ends securely with string to form a cracker shape. Make a string handle across the top. Lower the suet roll into the pan of boiling water and boil for 2 hours.

7 Using the string handle, lift the Spotted Dick out of the water. Put on a wire rack standing over a plate and allow the excess moisture to drain off.

8 Snip the string and gently roll the pudding out of the cloth or foil on to a warmed serving plate. Serve sliced with custard.

Sticky Toffee Puddings

Serves 4
Preparation Time
20 minutes
Cooking Time
25–30 minutes,
plus resting

Per Serving
565 calories
38g fat
(of which 21g saturates)
53g carbohydrate
0.9g salt

Vegetarian

1 tbsp golden syrup
1 tbsp black treacle
150g (5oz) butter, softened
25g (1oz) pecan nuts or walnuts, finely ground
75g (3oz) self-raising flour
125g (4oz) caster sugar
2 large eggs, beaten
cream or custard to serve

1 Preheat the oven to 180°C (160°C fan oven) mark 4. Put the syrup, treacle and 25g (1oz) of the butter into a bowl and beat until smooth. Divide the mixture among four 150ml (¼ pint) timbales or ramekins and set aside.

2 Put the nuts into a bowl, sift in the flour and mix together well.

3 Put the remaining butter and the sugar into a food processor and whiz briefly. (Alternatively, use a hand-held electric whisk.) Add the eggs and the flour mixture and whiz or mix again for 30 seconds. Spoon the mixture into the timbales or ramekins, to cover the syrup mixture. Bake for 25–30 minutes until risen and golden.

4 Remove the puddings from the oven and leave to rest for 5 minutes, then unmould on to warmed plates. Serve immediately with cream or custard.

Apple Crumble

Serves 4
Preparation Time
15 minutes
Cooking Time
45 minutes

Per Serving
425 calories
18g fat
(of which 7g saturates)
74g carbohydrate
0.3g salt

Vegetarian

125g (4oz) plain flour
50g (2oz) unsalted butter, cubed
50g (2oz) golden caster sugar
450g (1lb) apples, peeled, cored and sliced
vanilla custard or double cream to serve

1 Preheat the oven to 180°C (160°C fan oven) mark 4.
Put the flour into a bowl, add the butter and rub in
with your fingertips until the mixture resembles fine
breadcrumbs. Stir in half the sugar. Put to one side.

2 Arrange half the apples in a 1.1 litre (2 pint) pie dish
and sprinkle with the rest of the sugar. Add the
remaining apple slices to the dish. Spoon the crumble
mixture over the fruit.

3 Bake for 45 minutes or until the fruit is soft. Serve hot
with custard or a drizzle of double cream.

Lemon Meringue Pie

Serves 8
Preparation Time
30 minutes,
plus chilling
Cooking Time
about 1 hour,
plus standing

Per serving
692 calories
36g fat
(of which 21g saturates)
83g carbohydrate
0.6g salt

Vegetarian

Sweet pastry
225g (8oz) plain flour , plus extra to dust
pinch of salt
150g (5oz) butter, cut into pieces
2 tbsp caster sugar
1 medium egg yolk
3 tbsp cold water
a little beaten egg, to brush

For the filling and topping
7 medium eggs, 4 separated, at
room temperature
finely grated zest of 3 lemons
175ml (6fl oz) freshly squeezed lemon juice
(about 4 lemons), strained
400g can condensed milk
150ml (¼ pint) double cream
225g (8oz) golden icing sugar

1 To make the pastry, put the flour and salt into a bowl. Rub the fat into the flour until the mixture resembles breadcrumbs. Stir in the sugar. Mix the egg yolk with the water, then add to the dry ingredients, stirring with a round-bladed knife until the ingredients begin to stick together in lumps. With one hand collect the mixture together and knead for a few seconds to give a smooth dough. Wrap in clingfilm and chill for 30 minutes.

2 Roll out the pastry on a lightly floured surface and use to line a 23cm (9in), 4cm (1½in) deep, loose-based fluted tart tin. Prick the base with a fork and chill for 30 minutes. Meanwhile, preheat the oven to 190°C (170°C fan oven) mark 5.

3 Cover the pastry case with foil or greaseproof paper 8cm (3¼in) larger than the tin and spread baking beans or dried pulses on top. Bake blind for 10 minutes. Remove the foil or paper and beans and bake for a further 10 minutes. Brush the inside with beaten egg and put back in the oven for 1 minute to seal. Increase the oven setting to 180°C (160°C fan oven) mark 4.

4 To make the filling, put 4 egg yolks into a bowl with the 3 whole eggs. Add the lemon zest and juice, and whisk lightly. Mix in the condensed milk and cream.

5 Pour the filling into the pastry case and bake for 30 minutes or until just set in the centre. Set aside to cool while you prepare the meringue. Increase the oven setting to 200°C (180°C fan oven) mark 6 .

6 For the meringue, whisk the egg whites and icing sugar together in a heatproof bowl set over a pan of gently simmering water, using a hand-held electric whisk, for 10 minutes or until shiny and thick. Take off the heat and continue to whisk at low speed for 5–10 minutes until the bowl is cool. Pile the meringue on to the filling and swirl to form peaks. Bake for 5–10 minutes until the meringue is tinged brown. Leave to stand for about 1 hour, then serve.

Try something different
Use lime zest and juice instead of lemon.

Treacle Tart

Cuts into 6 slices

Preparation Time
25 minutes,
plus chilling

Cooking Time
45–50 minutes,
plus cooling

Per Slice
486 calories
15g fat
(of which 8g saturates)
88g carbohydrate
1.1g salt

Vegetarian

Sweet pastry
225g (8oz) plain flour, plus extra to dust
150g (5oz) unsalted butter
15g (½oz) golden caster sugar
1 medium egg yolk

For the filling
700g (1½lb) golden syrup
175g (6oz) fresh white breadcrumbs
grated zest of 3 lemons
2 medium eggs, lightly beaten

1 To make the pastry, sift the flour into a mound on a clean surface. Make a large well in the centre, add the butter, sugar and egg yolk. Using the fingertips of one hand, work the sugar, butter and egg yolk together until well blended. Gradually work in all the flour to bind the mixture together. Knead the dough gently on a lightly floured surface until smooth, then wrap in clingfilm and leave to rest in the fridge for 30 minutes.

2 Preheat the oven to 180°C (160°C fan oven) mark 4. Roll out the pastry on a lightly floured surface and use to line a 25.5cm (10in), 4cm (1½in) deep, loose-based fluted tart tin. Prick the base all over with a fork and chill for 30 minutes.

3 To make the filling, heat the syrup in a pan over a low heat until thinner in consistency. Remove from the heat and mix in the breadcrumbs and lemon zest. Stir in the beaten eggs.

4 Pour the filling into the pastry case and bake for 45–50 minutes until the filling is lightly set and golden. Allow to cool slightly. Serve warm.

Try something different
For the pastry, replace half the plain flour with wholemeal flour. For the filling, use fresh wholemeal breadcrumbs instead of white.

Quick Chocolate Slices

Makes 40

Preparation Time
10 minutes

Cooking Time
2 minutes

Per Slice
137 calories
9.3g fat
(of which 5.5g saturates)
12.7g carbohydrate
0.3g salt

Vegetarian

225g (8oz) butter or olive oil spread, plus extra to grease
3 tbsp golden syrup
50g (2oz) cocoa, sifted
300g pack digestive biscuits, crushed
400g (14oz) plain chocolate (at least 70 per cent cocoa solids), broken into pieces

1 Put the butter or olive oil spread in a bowl and add the golden syrup and cocoa. Melt in a 900W microwave on High for 20 seconds or until melted. Alternatively, melt in a pan over a very low heat. Mix everything together.

2 Remove from the heat and stir in the biscuits. Mix well until thoroughly coated in chocolate, crushing down any large pieces of biscuit.

3 Turn into a greased 25.5 × 16.5cm (10 × 6½in) rectangular tin. Cool, cover and chill for 20 minutes.

4 Melt the chocolate in a heatproof bowl in a 900W microwave on High for 1 minute 40 seconds, stirring twice. Alternatively, melt over a pan of gently simmering water. Stir once more and pour over the chocolate biscuit base, then chill for 20 minutes. Cut in half lengthways and cut each half into 20 rectangular fingers.

Index

KITCHEN NOTES

Both metric and imperial measures are given for the recipes. Follow either set of measures, not a mixture of both, as they are not interchangeable.

All spoon measures are level.
1 tsp = 5ml spoon; 1 tbsp = 15ml spoon.

Ovens and grills must be preheated to the specified temperature.

Medium eggs should be used except where otherwise specified. Free-range eggs are recommended.

Note that some recipes contain raw or lightly cooked eggs. The young, elderly, pregnant women and anyone with an immune-deficiency disease should avoid these because of the slight risk of salmonella.

Photographers: Neil Barclay (pages 5, 8, 9, 16, 17, 36, 53 and 94); Steve Baxter (pages 26 & 27); Martin Brigdale (page 19); Nicki Dowey (pages 6, 7, 12, 18, 20, 21, 25, 43, 52, 60, 62, 63, 68, 69, 70, 73, 74, 75, 84, 85, 88, 89 and 96); Will Heap (pages 40 & 41); Fiona Kennedy (pages 14, 34, 35, 64 and 65); Gareth Morgans (pages 44 & 45); Craig Robertson (pages 13, 15, 22, 53, 37, 38, 39, 54, 55, 58, 59, 66, 67, 71, 76, 77, 78, 79, 80, 82, 83 and 92); Brett Stevens (pages 56 & 57); Lucinda Symons (pages 10, 11, 24, 28, 29, 30, 31, 32, 33, 42, 46, 47, 48, 49, 50, 51, 72, 81, 86, 87, 90, 91 and 93)

Home Economists: Joanna Farrow, Emma Jane Frost, Teresa Goldfinch, Alice Hart, Lucy McKelvie, Kim Morphew, Aya Nishimura, Bridget Sargeson, Kate Trend and Mari Mererid Williams
Stylists: Tamzin Ferdinando, Wei Tang, Helen Trent and Fanny Ward

First published in Great Britain in 2012
by Collins & Brown
10 Southcombe Street
London W14 0RA

An imprint of Anova Books Company Ltd

The Good Housekeeping website is
www.allaboutyou.com/goodhousekeeping

ISBN 978-1-908449-30-6

A catalogue record for this book is available from the British Library.

Reproduction by Dot Gradations Ltd, UK
Printed and bound by 1010 Printing International Ltd, China

This book can be ordered direct from the publisher. Contact the marketing department, but try your bookshop first.

www.anovabooks.com